The Open University

Mathematics and Computing/Technology
An Inter-faculty Second Level Course

MT262 Putting Computer Systems to Work

Block I
Beginnings

Unit 2
Problem Solving

Prepared for the Course Team by Alan Best

This text forms part of the Open University second-level course MT262 *Putting Computer Systems to Work*, which among other things teaches the use of Borland C^{++}Builder 5 Standard to tackle small programming projects. (Borland C^{++}Builder 5 Standard is copyright © 2000 Borland International (UK) Limited.)

The course software comprises the Borland C^{++}Builder 5 Standard CD-ROM and the MT262 Templates and Libraries CD-ROM, both of which are supplied as part of the course.

This publication forms part of an Open University course. Details of this and other Open University courses can be obtained from the Student Registration and Enquiry Service, The Open University, PO Box 197, Milton Keynes, MK7 6BJ, United Kingdom: tel. +44 (0)870 333 4340, e-mail general-enquiries@open.ac.uk

Alternatively, you may visit the Open University website at http://www.open.ac.uk where you can learn more about the wide range of courses and packs offered at all levels by The Open University.

To purchase a selection of Open University course materials, visit the webshop at www.ouw.co.uk, or contact Open University Worldwide, Michael Young Building, Walton Hall, Milton Keynes, MK7 6AA, United Kingdom, for a brochure: tel. +44 (0)1908 858785, fax +44 (0)1908 858787, e-mail ouwenq@open.ac.uk

The Open University, Walton Hall, Milton Keynes, MK7 6AA.

First published 1999. Second edition 2002.

Edited, designed and typeset by The Open University, using the Open University TEX System.

Printed in the United Kingdom by Martins the Printers, Berwick-upon-Tweed

ISBN 0 7492 4038 5

2.2

Contents

Study guide

A recommended study pattern, based on an average overall study time, is as follows. Study times for the sections are expected to be roughly equal.

Material	Study time
Introduction, Section 1 (computer)	$2\frac{1}{2}$ hours
Section 2 (text)	$2\frac{1}{2}$ hours
Section 3 (text)	$2\frac{1}{2}$ hours
Section 4 (computer)	$2\frac{1}{2}$ hours
Section 5 (computer)	$2\frac{1}{2}$ hours

You will need access to your computer whilst studying Sections 1, 4 and 5.

The material in Section 2 is intended to be read lightly at this stage. It contains a survey of some types of data used in designing and coding solutions. You are likely to make further use of it as reference material later.

In many cases, the course team's solutions to computer activities are provided as computer files. They were installed when you installed the MT262 Templates and Libraries software. The course team will usually follow the convention of naming its solution file for a programming project by placing CT before the suggested name of that project. Thus, if you worked on a project with suggested name Mean1 in the text, the solution will be found in CTMean1. All files are placed in the appropriate subfolder of the MT262 folder. The files required in this unit are in MT262\Block I.

From now on, the exercises and computer activities form an essential part of the course material. Some provide practice in ideas introduced in the text; some actually introduce new ideas. In all cases it is very important to check the solution provided, even if you are totally happy with yours. There may well be points made in the solution that you might otherwise overlook.

Introduction

The challenge of using a computer to solve a given problem can be quite daunting, and the student new to this discipline inevitably needs help to get started. As in many walks of life, one gets better with practice and experience, and that process starts in this unit. There are no hard and fast rules for how to get involved in problem solving, and all that is given in this course are some guidelines and strategies for a general approach, together with suggestions of things to try when no progress is being made.

As you work through the examples you will see how to make a start on a problem: by looking at the problem in a global way, and then gradually breaking it down into smaller and smaller components that can be tackled separately. This way of solving problems is known as a **top-down** approach.

If you cannot make headway with a problem, a recommended approach is to try to solve a simplified version of the problem first. Experiences gained from solving the simpler version could well suggest approaches to the more complex problem. In a sense, that is exactly what is done in this unit. A very simple problem is used to introduce you to design ideas and to writing C++ programs that implement the design. Throughout the unit you will move on to more complicated versions of the same problem, and meet more design and coding ideas. By the end of this unit, you should be able to design, code and hence solve simple, but non-trivial, problems with the aid of the computer.

Section 1 introduces a simple version of the problem of finding the mean (average) of a collection of numbers. The problem is used to illustrate the top-down approach for designing solutions. It also introduces a number of design concepts and the way in which these are expressed in C++.

In Section 2 you will look at the kinds of data that computers might be called upon to handle in order to solve problems. At the same time, the operations that can be carried out on such data are discussed. Alongside the design aspects of data, you will see how data and the operations on it are expressed in C++.

Sections 3 and 4 explore extensions of the original mean-finding problem and, as a result, introduce new design ideas and the corresponding C++ code for these ideas.

Finally, Section 5 invites you to go through the whole design and coding process for a new problem. As it is the first such exercise in the course, it is broken down into a series of steps, with guidance on what you should do at each stage.

From time to time there are references to **ANSI**, which is the acronym for the **A**merican **N**ational **S**tandards **I**nstitute. ANSI sets standards in a large number of different fields, including programming languages. The (approximate) UK equivalent is the British Standards Institution (BSI).

1 Program design

In this section a problem is introduced that will be used to illustrate the course approach to designing and coding solutions. To begin with, the problem is very limited and its purpose is to introduce some key concepts. As extensions to the problem are investigated, you will see that the eventual solution is rather more useful.

1.1 A first design

We shall begin by designing a solution to a straightforward problem.

Problem Specification   Mean 1

A program is required whose purpose is to receive four numbers, and to write out their mean (average) value.   □

The first stage is to ensure that the problem specification is fully understood. The overall task may be clear, but there are some ambiguities that need to be resolved before the task can be started. The specification talks about the mean of four given numbers, but there are different kinds of number. There are positive and negative whole numbers like −3, 0, 11 and 237, called **integers**. There are also numbers with a decimal part such as 3.1417, 0.007 and −17.293, called **real numbers**. There are other kinds of numbers too, but these two types will suffice for the time being. As you will soon learn, the computer handles different types of number in different ways and so it is essential to know with what kind of number you are dealing.

To clear up the ambiguity over the numbers, let us suppose that the numbers to be averaged are whole numbers in the range 0 to 100 inclusive, such as the marks gained by a student on four assignments for an Open University course.

Clearing up ambiguities makes the specification more precise. This process is necessary for most initial problem specifications.

Exercise 1.1 _____

What type of number will the required mean be?

[*Solution on page 45*]

_____

You also need to know how the numbers which are to form the *input* to the program are to be provided. They might already be stored in the computer, or they could be provided in electronic form on a floppy disk. To keep things simple, let us suppose that the whole numbers are going to be supplied written on paper, so that the user (who is going to operate the keyboard) can key them in one after the other. As to *output* from the program, the mean value has to be written out. There are several possibilities, including using a printer, but to tie things down suppose that the output is to be written to the monitor screen.

The problem now seems to be specified clearly enough to move on to devising a solution. There appear to be three stages: an input stage at which the user enters four numbers from the keyboard; a processing stage at which the mean of the numbers is calculated; and an output stage at which the required mean is written to the monitor screen. This observation provides the following **top-level design**.

A top-level design should show the minimum amount of detail consistent with giving the basic structure of the solution.

1   read in the four numbers
2   calculate the mean of the four numbers
3   write out the mean

The top-down design strategy regards these three design steps as separate tasks. They are not entirely independent tasks, because the results from step 1, namely the numbers read in, are needed by step 2 as data with which it works. Similarly, step 2 provides a result which step 3 needs. Nevertheless, accepting that there will be data that the steps must share, we shall regard the three steps as separate subproblems.

Some thought must be given to the numbers forming the input to the program. They arrive as whole numbers written on paper, and then are typed at the keyboard. At this point the machine takes control of them. How are these numbers stored in the machine so that they can subsequently be accessed? The way this is done is through the use of **variables**, each with its **identifier**. For example, suppose that in some program we use the identifier *NextNumber* as a label for some integer to be entered from the keyboard. The design step for this purpose will be

   read in *NextNumber*

The visual model of variables as wipe-clean boards introduced in *Unit 1* can be used to explain what this design step does. The identifier is the label written on the board by which the data can be found.

The first entry on the board records the type of the variable.

When an identifier is used in a design or program, you can think of one board becoming the property of that identifier and the data on it being the *current* value associated with that identifier. So, if the value 26 is entered in response to the above design step, the value 26 will be written on the board earmarked for *NextNumber*. In the illustration below, further identifiers *SomeInteger* and *Count* have current values 39 and 3, respectively.

The value 26 replaces whatever value was on the board previously.

integer		integer		integer
NextNumber		*SomeInteger*		*Count*
26		39		3

Instructions written in steps of a program design may cause the value associated with an identifer to change. For example, the design step

   increment *Count* by 1

would result in the value on the board called *Count* being increased by 1, as illustrated below.

integer		integer		integer
NextNumber		*SomeInteger*		*Count*
26		39		4

The value on a board may be referenced (used) without changing its value. For example, the design step

    set *SomeInteger* equal to 2 times *NextNumber*

would not affect the value on the board of *NextNumber*, but would use this value, currently 26, in determining the value 2 times 26, namely 52, which becomes the current value on the board of *SomeInteger*, as shown below.

The previous value, 39, of *SomeInteger* is now lost.

integer		integer		integer
NextNumber		*SomeInteger*		*Count*
26		52		4

This analogy can be taken one stage further. The design step

    set *Ratio* equal to *NextNumber* divided by *Count*

would require another board for the variable with identifier *Ratio*. The value that this step would assign, namely 6.5, is not a whole number and so the variable with identifier *Ratio* is not an integer variable. It is a real variable, as indicated on the board below.

real
Ratio
6.5

The fact that the values on the boards can vary in these ways is the reason for talking about variables and referring to the identifiers as the names of those variables. In an actual computer, the boards are blocks of memory, and the identifiers are memory addresses which the compiler uses to create instructions to retrieve or update the values held in these blocks of memory. Unlike the diagrams, the blocks of memory may not all be the same size. Telling the compiler the type of the data to be stored ensures that the correct amount of memory is reserved, and the binary patterns in that memory are correctly interpreted as an integer, a real number or whatever has been asked for. Variables, and the types of value they can take, are discussed in Section 2. From now on, the precise phrase 'the variable with identifier *Ratio*' will be contracted to 'the variable *Ratio*'.

The size of memory block for a given type of data depends on both the computer system involved *and* the particular compiler, even for the same language, say C++. The ANSI standard for C++ merely says that the manuals should provide the information.

Returning to the problem of calculating a mean value, what variables are needed? The course team saw five variables in this problem, but there is no 'correct' answer to this question; design is an individual art, and you may be thinking of developing one or more of the three design steps in a different way from the course team.

Exercise 1.2

Draw up a list of variables which you think are going to figure in a solution to this problem, giving each an appropriate identifier and saying what type of variable it is.

[*Solution on page 45*]

The five variables introduced in the solution to the previous exercise are noted in the following **data table**. For each variable, this table displays the type of data stored, its identifier and a brief description of the role.

Type	Identifier	Description
Integer	*First*	The first number entered from the keyboard
Integer	*Second*	The second number entered from the keyboard
Integer	*Third*	The third number entered from the keyboard
Integer	*Fourth*	The fourth number entered from the keyboard
Real	*Mean*	The mean value of the four numbers entered

The first attempt at a data table for a problem solution will often not be the final table. As the design develops, the need for further variables will arise and, conversely, it might happen that the need for one or more of the original variables disappears as things begin to take shape. However, thinking about the data at an early stage in a problem is important. Each step in the finished design will involve manipulation of some data, and identifying that data is a major step on the road to deciding how it is to be manipulated. Hence, producing a provisional data table is a significant step along to the road to a solution.

1.2   Refining the design

Having identified three separate tasks in the design and having spelled out the data with which they are to be concerned, any step can be tackled first. On this occasion, let us start at the beginning, with step 1.

1   read in the four numbers

This certainly divides into four separate subtasks, namely read in the first number, then read in the second, then the third and finally the fourth. The refined design reflecting this is as follows.

1.1   read in *First*
1.2   read in *Second*
1.3   read in *Third*
1.4   read in *Fourth*

Take careful note of the numbering that is being used. For instance, step 1.3 identifies the third step in the refinement of step 1. Also note that the appropriate variables from the data table appear in the design. Thus, for example, from now on references are to *Third* and not to 'third number'. One goal of a finished design is that each design step must be concerned with standard operations on identifiers in the data table; all descriptions of variables and operations on them should have vanished.

Exercise 1.3 _____
Refine step 3 of the top-level design

3   write out the mean

so that the data table decisions are incorporated.

[*Solution on page 45*]

_____

Contrary to what you may be thinking, steps 1 and 3 are not yet completed, as a little further work is necessary. But for the moment, consider the processing step.

2   calculate the mean of the four numbers

If *you* were given four numbers and were asked for their mean value, what would you do? You would add up the four numbers and divide the total by 4. Step 2 can be developed on those lines.

2.1   set *Mean* to the sum of the four numbers divided by 4

This step is deliberately written in English, mixing variable identifiers and prose. It conveys exactly what is to be done, but it is a long way removed from being an instruction that the machine could comprehend. This is an example of an **assignment step**, whereby a value is *assigned* to a variable. In the *design* language used in the course, assignment steps are written in the following way.

> *VariableIdentifier* ← Value

Assignment is a key concept in the style of programming used in MT262.

The symbol ← can be read as 'receives' or 'is assigned'. The variable on its left receives the value on its right. What appears to the left of ← in an assignment step must be a variable identifier. What appears to its right must be something giving a value of the correct type. For instance, if *MyReal* and *YourReal* are identifiers of two variables of type real, and *MyInteger* is an identifier of a variable of type integer, then each of the following is a valid assignment step. (Recall from *Unit 1* that '*', in the third assignment, denotes multiplication, and that, for clarity, spaces are placed around operators.)

> *MyReal* ← 3.1412
> *MyReal* ← *YourReal*
> *MyReal* ← (*YourReal* + 1.45) * 2.73
> *MyReal* ← *MyInteger*

In the first of these steps, a **constant** value is assigned to *MyReal*. In the second, the current value of a variable is assigned; after this assignment, *MyReal* and *YourReal* are not related in any way other than having the same current value. In the third step the value of an expression is assigned: the calculation on the right, which involves the current value of *YourReal*, is first performed, and the answer is the value assigned to *MyReal*.

If either *MyReal* or *YourReal* has its value changed subsequently, the other does *not* automatically change to match.

The fourth assignment is rather different. The expression on the right of the assignment symbol will yield an integer. This may be assigned to a real value by regarding the decimal part as being all zeros. The opposite action, assigning a real value to an integer variable, is fraught with difficulties. Should the real value have its decimal part discarded, or rounded, or what? Programming languages differ in what they do, with some not permitting such assignments at all. Since the *design* of solutions is intended to be as widely applicable as possible, assignments of real values to integer variables will *not* be permitted in our designs.

Exercise 1.4 _____

Write out the design step 2.1 in terms of identifiers.
(The above examples of assignment steps should help you to obtain the correct expression to be assigned to *Mean*.)

[Solution on page 45]

_____

If you put all the parts together, you are getting close to a complete design. However, if this design as it stands were to be coded and you were to run the program, you would realise immediately that something is missing. The program would present a blank screen. If the user happened to know that the program was waiting for four numbers to be input, and happened to know that the number it subsequently wrote out was their mean, then the program would just about be usable, though not by a stranger. The moral is that whenever a program requires input, the user should be prompted to provide it. Likewise, when a program sends results to the screen, the results ought to be accompanied by enough text messages to advise the user what the output is.

Thus step 1.1 must be refined further. A suitable refinement is as follows.

1.1.1 write out "Enter first number: "
1.1.2 read in *First*

What appears between double quotes will be written on screen *exactly* as it is typed. If punctuation is appropriate, then it should be included. For example, when prompting for the first number in step 1.1.1,

    "Enter first number: "

has been used. The colon and the space will improve the appearance on the screen. The expression to be written out in step 1.1.1 is a **string constant**. (A constant is a little like a variable, in that a board, or block of memory, is reserved for it. Unlike a variable, the contents of the board cannot be altered.) Data of type string is arguably one of the most important in computing. We shall look at it in detail in the next section, when string variables are introduced. For our present purposes, note that in just the same way as integers have values like 23, and real numbers have values like 3.1417, strings have values like "The cat sat on the mat" or "$23.00". A string value is distinguished from text by enclosing it in double quotes.

Carrying out similar refinements to the other substeps of step 1 and adding some explanatory text to the output in step 3, we reach our final design.

1.1.1 write out "Enter first number: "
1.1.2 read in *First*
1.2.1 write out "Enter second number: "
1.2.2 read in *Second*
1.3.1 write out "Enter third number: "
1.3.2 read in *Third*
1.4.1 write out "Enter fourth number: "
1.4.2 read in *Fourth*
2.1   *Mean* ← (*First* + *Second* + *Third* + *Fourth*)/4
3.1   write out "The mean value is "
3.2   write out *Mean*

Ideally, input and output requirements should be in the problem specification, but they are often left to the designer.

Steps 1.1.1 and 1.1.2 are the first and second steps in the refinement of step 1.1. As it happens, step 1.1.2 is the same as step 1.1.

Note that some steps are at the first refinement stage, and some are at the second.

No additional variables have been needed, so the provisional data table is also the final data table for this design. No further refinement is needed in order to translate this design into C++ code, as you will see in the next subsection. Any design that is ready for coding is called a **final design**.

1.3 Coding the design

When a design is in final form, the coding stage should prove to be relatively straightforward. There are plenty of opportunities for introducing errors while coding, as you will no doubt learn through experience, but many major errors in programming happen at the design stage.

Various types of error and how they arise are discussed in *Unit 4*.

The final design is simple in the sense that it comprises a single sequence of steps. Following the design manually involves starting at step 1.1.1 and progressing through the steps in sequence to step 3.2. The corresponding C++ code will, likewise, be a single sequence of **statements**. This is referred to as the 'main body of the C++ code' because the complete coded program involves a little more than the coding of the design steps.

Think of a statement as being a single coded instruction.

The code for our final design is as follows. Have a brief look through it to see how it matches with the design. Then read the discussion that follows.

```
int First;
int Second;
int Third;
int Fourth;
float Mean;
   First = ReadIntPr("Enter first number: ");
   Second = ReadIntPr("Enter second number: ");
   Third = ReadIntPr("Enter third number: ");
   Fourth = ReadIntPr("Enter fourth number: ");
   Mean = (First + Second + Third + Fourth)/4;
   WriteFloatPr("The mean value is ", Mean);
```

Ignoring the first five lines of this code, you may well have been able to relate the sequence of design steps coded in the remaining six lines to the design. But what are those first five lines in the code? The answer is that they are the coding of the data table. If a program is to use variables, then it needs to know about them: it has to be given the identifiers and the corresponding types. The first line of the code **declares** an integer variable. The word **int** is used in C++ to stand for *integer type*, and on this line what follows **int** is the name of the first integer variable to be used in the program. The next three lines declare the remaining integer variables. (It is permitted to combine declarations in C++, as indicated in point 2 below, but the course team feels quite strongly that the closer the code is to the design, the fewer errors you are likely to introduce in the translation from design to code. Hence, as above, you should give each variable declaration its own line.)

Exercise 1.5 ⎯⎯⎯⎯⎯⎯⎯⎯⎯⎯⎯⎯⎯⎯⎯⎯⎯⎯⎯⎯⎯⎯⎯⎯⎯⎯⎯⎯

What do you now understand by the fifth line in the code?

[*Solution on page 45*]

Before looking at other individual statements, there are three general observations to make.

1. Each statement, including the last one, finishes with a semicolon.

2. The program does not have to be laid out as neatly as presented here. The use of spacing and line breaks is an attempt to keep the code readable. The same program could be written as follows.

```
int First, Second, Third, Fourth;          float Mean;
First = ReadIntPr("Enter first number: ");Second =
ReadIntPr("Enter second number: ");Third
= ReadIntPr("Enter third number: ");Fourth =
ReadIntPr("Enter fourth number: ");Mean = (First
 + Second +
Third + Fourth)/4
;
WriteFloatPr("The mean value is ", Mean);
```

The course team hopes that you prefer the first version, for the reasons given above. Other programs will be laid out with the same care, and you are expected to do the same. This is not just a fad — the more readable your program code is, the more likely you are to be able to uncover errors.

3. The distinction between lower- and upper-case letters is crucial; C++ is case-sensitive. For example, when you type this program, you must not use *first* or *ReadintPr*, because the compiler will not recognise these as being the same as *First* and *ReadIntPr*.

Look now at the **assignment statement**

```
Mean = (First + Second + Third + Fourth)/4;
```

It is exactly as in the design except that the design assignment symbol, ←, has been replaced by '='. In C++ '=' is the assignment operator, and a C++ assignment statement takes the form

```
Variable = Value;
```

where, as you have seen with assignments in design, the value on the right-hand side can arise in a number of ways:

o   a constant value;

o   the current value of some variable;

o   an expression involving variables and arithmetic operations.

Different programming languages use a variety of different symbols for the assignment operator. You must be very careful in writing and reading C++ code to remember that the symbol '=' does *not* mean 'is equal to'.

C++ uses the double equals sign, '==', for 'is equal to'.

There are four other assignment statements, of the same type, in the code. For example, the statement

```
First = ReadIntPr("Enter first number: ");
```

is coding for the following pair of design steps.

1.1.1 write out "Enter first number: "
1.1.2 read in *First*

Here a value is assigned to variable *First*, but the value being assigned has first to be read from the keyboard. The instruction `ReadIntPr(...)` is one that you will quickly get used to using. It tells the computer to **Read** an **Int**eger value from the keyboard in response to the given **Pr**ompt. It is used in the following way.

Like many of the instructions available in C++, this is not part of the core language, but supplied in a code library. Some of the code libraries are supplied with all C++ systems; some have been produced for MT262. This instruction is in an MT262 library.

```
IntegerVariable = ReadIntPr("Prompt goes here");
```

There is, available for your use, a suite of such instructions for reading data from the keyboard and writing data to the screen. Such instructions are examples of **functions**; other functions will be introduced as you need them.

The one remaining statement in the code that has not yet been mentioned,

All the read and write functions are listed in the Handbook.

```
WriteFloatPr("The mean is: ", Mean);
```

might now be self-explanatory. The instruction `WriteFloatPr(...)` is to **Write** the given **Float** (i.e. real) value to the screen preceded by the given **Pr**ompt. The prompt and the real value, in this case the value of a variable, are listed in that order, in the accompanying (round) brackets.

Strictly speaking, 'round brackets' are 'parentheses', but they will be referred to as just 'brackets'.

That completes the discussion of the program. If you found it a lot to take in, do not worry; these ideas will grow on you rapidly as you gain experience through writing simple programs. Before you go to your PC to try out the program in the next subsection, attempt the following exercise, which reviews some of the notions that have just been discussed.

Exercise 1.6

Study the following C++ code, and then answer the questions about it that follow.

```
int MyInt;
int YourInt;
 YourInt = ReadIntPr("Enter any whole number: ");
 MyInt = YourInt + 6;
 WriteIntPr("I chose ... ", MyInt);
 WriteString(" ... my number is bigger so I win again!");
```

(a) What variables are declared? Describe them.

(b) What is read in from the keyboard? How is it processed?

(c) Why does the machine always win?

[*Solution on page 46*]

1.4 Running the program

The time has come to run the program implementing the design.

Computer Activity 1.1 _____

Carry out the following steps.

(a) Start Builder by using the shortcut icon that you set up in *Unit 1*. After a while you should be looking at the main Builder menu with just the Object Inspector and Code Editor windows open.

(b) Open a new console application. (Do this as you did in *Unit 1*. From the main menu, select `File|New...` and, in the resulting 'New Items' dialog box, double-click on the `Console Wizard` icon. In the 'Console Wizard' dialog box, make sure that `Console Application`, `Use VCL` and `C++` are checked and then click on `OK`. (If there are unsaved changes to what you were working on, you will be prompted to save them.))

> In future, the instruction 'Open a new console application' means carry out all the steps in the sentences in brackets.

If you wish, you can close the Object Inspector window and resize the Code Editor window (which should contain the page `Unit1.cpp`) to give yourself more room in which to work.

(c) Use `File|Save Project As...` to save the new project in the `Block I` subfolder of MT262. Use the names `Mean1U` for the unit file and `Mean1` for the project file. (You need not give the extensions — the parts of the names after the full stop — since Builder will automatically add the correct ones.)

(d) As in *Unit 1*, you need to make the MT262 course library available. Use `Project|Add to Project...` (or the 'speed button' with the file and the green '+' sign) and enter `MT262io.lib` for the requested file name and then click on `Open`.

Add the line

```
#include "MT262io.h"
```

just before the line

```
#pragma hdrstop
```

> The Code Editor should look like the figure below.

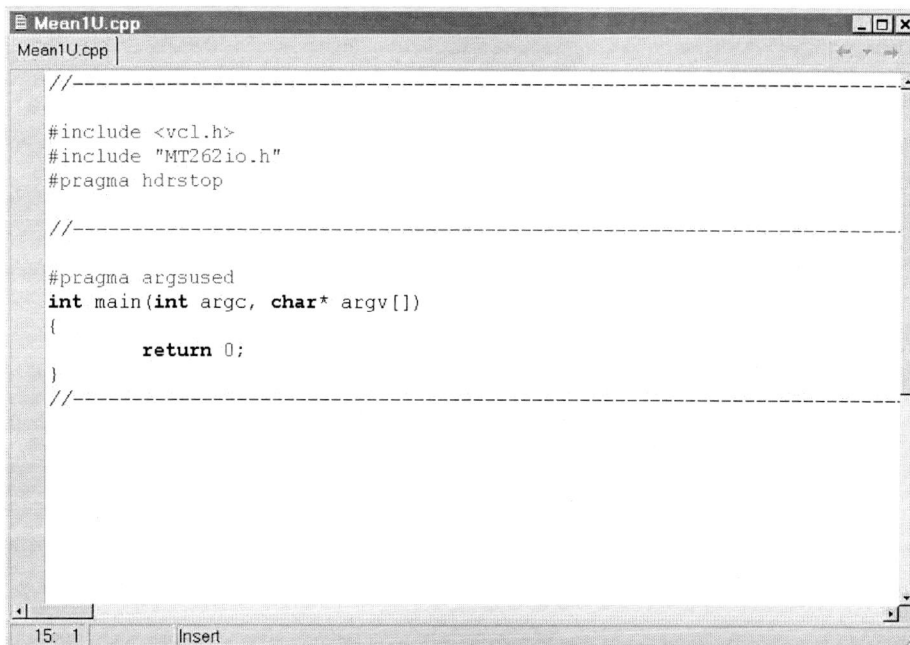

```
//---------------------------------------------------------------

#include <vcl.h>
#include "MT262io.h"
#pragma hdrstop

//---------------------------------------------------------------

#pragma argsused
int main(int argc, char* argv[])
{
        return 0;
}
//---------------------------------------------------------------
```

(e) Now enter the program code so that the part after the comment line looks as follows.

```
#pragma argsused
int main(int argc, char* argv[])
{
int First;
int Second;
int Third;
int Fourth;
float Mean;
 First = ReadIntPr("Enter first number: ");
 Second = ReadIntPr("Enter second number: ");
 Third = ReadIntPr("Enter third number: ");
 Fourth = ReadIntPr("Enter fourth number: ");
 Mean = (First + Second + Third + Fourth)/4;
 WriteFloatPr("The mean value is ", Mean);
 getchar();
 return 0;
}
```

As in *Unit 1*, the statement `getchar();` has been added; the purpose of this is to hold the screen output until the Enter key is pressed.

(f) Run the program by choosing `Run|Run`. If you have typed everything correctly, your program will compile, link and run. If any errors are reported, try to correct them. The most likely causes of problems are misspelled words (particularly lower- and upper-case not being correct in identifiers) and omitting semicolons at the ends of statements. The error messages at the bottom of the Code Editor will usually give a clue, but will often point to a place just *after* the error because that is when the compiler is able to detect that an error has occurred. If you really cannot fathom out what has gone wrong, you can open the course team's version of this program by using the `File|Open Project...` option from the main menu and opening the project `CTMean1.bpr`.

Note that when you select `Run` from the `Run` menu, Builder saves automatically whatever code you have entered since you last 'saved'.

(g) Run the program a few times, supplying your own data. Do not be too alarmed if you think the program is giving some strange answers! (Remember to close the program window by pressing `Enter` between each run.)

Leave the machine running if you are going on to the next computer activity.

[*Solution on page 53*]

One thing you ought to have noticed from running this program is that it gives wrong answers! For example, if you enter the four numbers 1, 2, 3 and 4, the program claims that the mean value is 2 rather than the 2.5 which one would expect. Indeed, you might also have noticed that the program returns only whole number answers.

So what is going wrong? It is not the machine being temperamental, and it is not a design fault! It is a well-hidden *coding* error that you might not spot until testing the program and finding that something unexpected is happening.

It might be more accurate to call it a C^{++} 'feature'!

The problem lies in the assignment statement

```
Mean = (First + Second + Third + Fourth)/4;
```

The expression on the right-hand side of the above statement involves adding four integer values and dividing the answer by 4. In C++ (and other languages), if you divide an integer by an integer, the machine *assumes* that you are dealing with integers and that you want an integer answer. It will give the *integer part* of the real answer.

When this assignment statement is executed, the expression on the right is first evaluated giving an integer answer. This integer is then assigned to the **float** variable *Mean*. That is not a problem. The compiler is happy to assign whole numbers to real variables, attaching a number of zeros after a decimal point.

To correct the code requires some way of informing the compiler that the division involved in that assignment statement is division of real numbers and not integer division. This is done by writing an instruction that tells the machine to treat the numerator in the division as a real number (albeit with a whole number value), by use of the keyword **float**:

```
Mean = float(First + Second + Third + Fourth)/4;
```

Now the expression on the right divides a real value by 4 and assigns the (real) answer to *Mean*. The next activity tries this correction.

Computer Activity 1.2 _____
Make the correction to your code for `Mean1` by adding the word **float** as indicated. Run the program again, and confirm that the calculations are now correct.

[*Solution on page 53*]

Before leaving this program, there is one more short experiment for you to try. The mean calculating program requests four integer values to be entered from the keyboard. Whilst testing the program, have you tried entering values that are not whole numbers? Try the following activity.

Computer Activity 1.3 _____
In response to a prompt for an integer, how does the program `Mean1` handle the following inputs?

(a) A real value such as 3.7.

(b) An alphanumeric character such as 'k'.

(c) The Enter key; that is, entering nothing.

[*Solution on page 53*]

The way in which such 'user errors' are to be handled *should* be part of the problem specification. In practice, most specifications are incomplete in this respect, not least because users invent ingenious errors!

2 Variables

From your work in the previous section, you should appreciate that a key concept in problem solving is that of the *variable*. Both the design and coding stages are principally concerned with storing and manipulating data, and data is accessed via variables through their identifiers.

You are reminded to treat this section as a light read, and refer to it as necessary in later units.

The previous section demonstrated some ways in which variables are used, but probably you were left with many questions about variables unanswered — for example, the following.

- What types of data items can be handled?
- What calculations or other operations can be performed on data?
- What values of data items can be handled?
- What identifiers (names) can be used in a program?

These questions will be addressed in this section.

2.1 Identifiers

A design should include a data table as a reminder of decisions about what data has to be processed and what identifiers will be used. As described in Section 1, a variable in a program is a part of the computer's memory, the contents of which can change as the program is run. So that the compiler will generate code to correctly manipulate data, it needs the information from the data table. This information is provided by **variable declarations**. There are two stages in declaring a variable:

- stating the type of the variable;
- choosing an identifier for the variable.

The phrase *data type* has a technical meaning which has rather fallen into disuse. Any phrase resembling this in MT262 simply has its everyday meaning: the nature of the data item — number, character, string, picture, sound, etc.

In choosing an identifier you should try to select something which reminds you of the purpose of the variable, so that the design and program are easier to read and understand. For example, *First* and *Mean* (of Section 1) are more meaningful identifiers than X and Z. Beyond this there are a few further rules to be applied. The following are the rules for C++, with comments.

- Identifiers can be up to 32 characters in length. (Actually, they can be any length, but the compiler takes notice of only the first 32 characters.)

At this stage, think of a character as something you can type at the keyboard.

- An identifier must begin with a letter (either upper- or lower-case). (Actually, C++ also allows use of the underscore character (_) in this position, but, for reasons that are buried in the history of C++, the course team never uses an underscore at the beginning of an identifier, and neither should you.)

- After the initial letter, subsequent characters may be letters, underscores, or the digits 0 to 9, but an identifier must not contain any other characters. (The underscore is traditionally used to run words together and have identifiers such as *Next_number*. The chosen style in this course is to avoid such use of the underscore; the cited example would be written as *NextNumber*.)

- Identifiers are case-sensitive; that is, for example, Index, index, INDEX and iNdeX are four different identifiers. (This is easy to forget about, and may be the cause of puzzling compiler errors.)

○ No **keyword** may be used as a variable identifier. Keywords are special identifiers which are reserved for particular roles in programs. You have already met the keywords **int** and **float**. You will meet some more, including **char**, **bool**, **while** and **if**, in this unit. (Any keyword typed in Builder's Code Editor window is automatically emboldened, so you should have no difficulty recognising them.)

There are over 50 keywords in all; you will meet about half of them in this course. Look in the Builder Help system for a complete list if you are interested. (Select Index from the Help menu, type keywords in box 1, select alphabetical listing in box 2, and then click on Display.)

These are the rules (modified by the comments) that will be adhered to in this course. It should be mentioned, however, that the rules governing identifiers are not standard in computing languages. For example, several languages impose the condition that identifiers are not case-sensitive. Because the names that result from the modified rules are legal in many languages, these rules will also be used for the design stage.

Exercise 2.1

Which of the following may be used as a variable identifier, and which may not?

*MyFirst, second, gross%, x_0, Item123, a_to_z, #pounds, my*program*

[*Solution on page 46*]

When declaring a variable you must also give its type. The type of a variable determines the set of values that the variable can take. There are many data types. There are standard (or built-in) types including **integer** and **real**. As you will see in Block II, there are other types which the designer can create. In the remainder of this section, the main standard types will be discussed. The set of values that each type can hold will be discussed, and the operations that can be performed with each indicated. This last point is important for several reasons. It is of little use to know that C^{++} can cope with integers in the range from $-2\,147\,483\,648$ to $2\,147\,483\,647$ if you do not also know that integers can be added, subtracted, multiplied, divided, compared, assigned, and so on.

The alternative description 'built-in' refers to the fact that these types are found built in to most programming languages.

A word of warning is in order here. The range of values that can be stored in each C^{++} data type is dependent on which C^{++} compiler you use. Compilers are often tailored to produce code that runs efficiently on a particular computer system. Thus a C^{++} compiler producing code intended for a washing machine controller may have ranges of values different from those in Builder. The ANSI standard for C^{++} merely demands that the compiler documentation describes the ranges. You will see what Builder provides, but you need to be aware that other systems may provide very different ranges.

The Builder Help system index has entries which set out in detail the range of values for different data types. It also describes the internal representation of types. Search for 'data types, 32-bit'.

2.2 Integers

Mathematically, the integers are the whole numbers, such as −23, 0, 17, and there is no limit to their size, either positive or negative. There has to be some limit to the size of integer a computer can store, even if one allocated all of the memory to storing a single integer!

The limit is dependent on the implementation. In Builder, a variable declared to be of type integer can take whole number values in the range from −2 147 483 648 to 2 147 483 647, which will be more than adequate for our purposes in this course. There are numerous operations that can be carried out on integers, including addition, subtraction and multiplication (for which the symbol * is used). So, for example, we can write expressions such as 17 + 3, 3 − 7 and 2 * 8. The values of these expressions are integer **constants**. Expressions involving integers can also be formed using integer variables.

For details, look in the Builder Help system index under 'constants, internal representation'.

Exercise 2.2

If *Total* is a variable of type integer whose current value is 12, what are the values of the following expressions?

(a) 3 * *Total*

(b) *Total* − 7 * *Total*

(c) (*Total* − 7) * *Total*

(d) *Total* * −5

[*Solution on page 46*]

There is also the operation of division, but this presents an added complication in that there are two ways of dividing integers. Once you had met decimal fractions in your school career, your answer to division of 5 by 2 would probably be 2.5. This form of division yields what has been referred to as a real number. However, C++ compilers are 'smart': they look at the data being operated on, and try to perform an operation to give a result *of the same type*. Thus (as you witnessed in the previous section) C++ would say that 5/2 is 2. This is, appropriately enough, called **integer division**. To calculate an integer division by hand, divide to obtain a real result, and then round to the integer towards zero. Thus, for example, integer division yields:

Before you met decimal fractions, division of 5 by 2 would probably have given the answer 2 (remainder 1).

$$(11/4) = 2, \quad \text{since 2.75 rounds (towards zero) to 2;}$$
$$(-11/4) = -2, \quad \text{since } -2.75 \text{ rounds (towards zero) to } -2.$$

There is another useful operation on integers, closely allied to integer division. The **remainder operator** yields the remainder in an integer division. For example, since 5 goes into 17 three times leaving remainder 2, the remainder of 17 on division by 5 is 2.

Programming languages differ in how they represent integer and real division and the remainder operator. At the design stage it is essential to distinguish whether a division is to produce a real or an integer result; this is done by using a special symbol 'div' for integer division. For the remainder operator in designs, the symbol that C++ uses, namely '%' will be used. These conventions are summarised below.

Several languages use 'mod' for the remainder operator.

At the *design* stage
- Division (with real result) is always denoted by '/'.
- Integer division is denoted by 'div'. Example:

    17 div 5 = 3.

- The remainder operator is denoted by '%'. Example:

    17 % 5 = 2.

In C^{++}
- Division is always denoted by '/', and the result will depend on the type of the numbers being operated on. Examples:

    $17/5 = 3$,
    $17.0/5 = 3.4$.

- The remainder operator is denoted by '%'. Example:

    17 % 5 = 2.

There is a set of comparison operators which can be applied to pairs of integer operands and which give values which are neither integer nor real: the values are **true** and **false**. As their name suggests, these operators, of which there are six, are used to compare the relative sizes of integers. For example, $1 + 2 > 2$ is true, whereas $2 < 2$ is false. The symbols $>$ and $<$ are used in C^{++} and at the design stage.

Comparison of other types is discussed later.

The following table shows all six comparison operators. At the design stage the usual mathematical symbol is used for each of them. The C^{++} symbols, particularly for equality and inequality, are unusual. As a reminder from the previous section, the assignment operator is included in the table as its C^{++} symbol is readily mistaken for equality.

Most other programming languages also use symbols close to the mathematical ones.

Design stage symbol	Meaning	C^{++} version
integer	integer	**int**
$\leftarrow$	assignment	$=$
$=$	is equal to	$==$
$\neq$	is not equal to	$!=$
$<$	is less than	$<$
$>$	is greater than	$>$
$\leq$	is less than or equal to	$<=$
$\geq$	is greater than or equal to	$>=$

Exercise 2.3

Determine the value of each of the following design stage expressions (comparisons), where *Total* is an integer variable whose current value is 12.

(a) $2 > 7$

(b) $9 \% 4 \geq 1$

(c) $3 * 4 \neq Total$

(d) $Total$ div $5 = 2$

[*Solution on page 46*]

You may have noticed that another data type has been introduced in this discussion of comparison operations: you have met expressions which can have one of two values, **true** or **false**. This type of data, comprising the two values {**true**, **false**} is known as the **boolean** data type, of which more in Subsection 2.6.

2.3 Real numbers

Real numbers are numbers like 3.0, 2.657, -22.71498, $+2.37$, which are written with digits on both sides of a decimal point and, optionally, a sign preceding the number. Just as with integers, there is a limit on the size of real number that a computer can handle. But it is not only size that matters with real numbers. There is also a restriction on the precision of the number — that is, on how many significant digits can be stored. For example, the number 1/3 has unending decimal 0.333333..., and to store this number as a real requires a decision on how many decimal places to retain.

The phrase 'a real number' is often contracted to 'a real'.

Computers invariably use what is known as **floating point representation** of real numbers. There is no need for you to appreciate fully what this entails; you can happily leave the machine to store and manipulate real numbers without knowing what is going on. But as you will come across floating point numbers in your practical work, it is as well that you have at least an awareness of them. Here is an example.

Consider the real number 597.43. The machine would store this as follows.

5.9743000000E2

The mathematical version of this is 5.9743000000×10^2.

The number to the left of the 'E' is the **mantissa** and the integer following the 'E' is the **exponent**. In general, the mantissa is a real number lying between 1 and 10, so that the decimal point is in second position. The exponent indicates the power of 10 by which to multiply the mantissa to recover the original version of the real number. In this case, the exponent 2 means multiply by 10 twice, or what amounts to the same thing, move the decimal point two places to the right. The mantissa has also had some 0s appended. The mantissa holds the significant digits of the real number, and how many there will be varies from compiler to compiler. In the illustration above, the mantissa is 12 characters in all, 11 significant digits plus the decimal point.

The exponent may be negative. For example, the number 0.00059743 would be stored as follows.

5.9743000000E−4

$5.9743000000 \times 10^{-4}$

To recover the real number from the floating point form requires the decimal point to be moved 4 places to the *left*, which involves adding 0s appropriately to the start of the mantissa to give 0.00059743.

In this course you are not going to deal with problems involving large real numbers, nor with problems requiring high precision. The only reason that you need a passing appreciation of the floating point representation is because you will have occasion to write out the values of real numbers. For example, if a program computes a percentage, then you probably would be happier seeing the result written out as 72.4 rather than as 7.2438170000E1. So you are going to have to learn how to format the output of real numbers, but that is a story for a later unit.

Addition, subtraction, multiplication, division, assignment and the six comparison operations are defined for reals just as for integers. For division we shall use the same symbol '/'; the division of a real by a real gives a real answer. So if *MyReal* is a real variable with current value 12.0, then the expression *MyReal*/5 would have value 2.4.

The operations 'div' and % are not applicable to real numbers.

One word of caution: be wary in using the equality comparison operator with reals, because of the precision problem. The (design) comparison

$$1.0/3.0 = 0.333333$$

would almost certainly evaluate to false when coded, while the value (true or false) of

Since 1/3 has an unending decimal expansion, the comparison *is* false!

$$1.0/10.0 = 0.1$$

cannot be predicted with confidence!

Exercise 2.4

Determine the value of each of the following expressions, where *First* and *Second* are real variables with current values 2.0 and 3.71, respectively.

(a) *First* $-$ 2 * *Second*

(b) *Second*/*First*

(c) *Second* $<$ 2 * *First*

[*Solution on page 47*]

Before moving on, there is an important point to make concerning the values that real variables can take. If *First* is a real variable, then the two assignments *First* $\leftarrow$ 3 and *First* $\leftarrow$ 3.0 are both valid, and have the same effect of assigning the real value equal to 3.0 to *First*. In general, because each integer is an example of a real number, integer values can be assigned to real variables. The opposite assignment is fraught with difficulties. If *Count* is an integer variable, what should the assignment *Count* $\leftarrow$ 3.0 do? One reasonable assumption is that *Count* should have the value 3, which is the integer part of 3.0. Unfortunately, programming languages differ in how they treat assignment to a more restricted type of variable. This type of assignment is best avoided at the design stage, where possible. How to make C^{++} do what is wanted will be discussed when it becomes necessary.

In the previous section you met the data type **float** for representing real numbers. A variable of this type is allocated 4 bytes of memory by Builder, and this provides a large enough range of real numbers with sufficient precision for most applications. However, there are alternatives. A variable of type **double** is allocated 8 bytes of memory by Builder for holding, in floating point form, the value of a real number. As its name suggests, the precision of the values will be effectively doubled.

In Builder, **double** provides much greater precision than **float**. The ANSI standard just requires that **double** shall provide at least as much precision as **float**, possibly more. If using other compilers, you would need to check the provision.

The following table summarises what you need to know about real numbers, and gives the C++ versions of the concepts.

Design stage symbol	Meaning	C++ version
real number	real number	**float**
real number	real number (greater precision)	**double**
+	addition	+
−	subtraction	−
*	multiplication	*
/	division	/
←	assignment	=
=	is equal to	==
≠	is not equal to	!=
<	is less than	<
>	is greater than	>
≤	is less than or equal to	<=
≥	is greater than or equal to	>=

2.4 Characters

Character data is the most commonly used data in communication between the user and the machine. Each computer system has an associated set of characters that it uses, which at a simplistic level one can think of as being all the different possible keypresses available from the computer keyboard. Unfortunately, different machines interpret some of the less common keypresses in different ways, so there is no universally agreed character set. In this course we shall use the ASCII character set. This includes all the standard keys that one would use in word-processing: the 52 roman letters (upper- and lower-case), the 10 digits, the punctuation symbols, and other symbols such as the addition symbol, the dollar sign and the space character. There are other members of the character set that have no associated symbol; these are referred to as 'non-printing' characters. For example, when reading from the keyboard, the machine associates the typing of the Escape key with one of its non-printing characters.

A character variable may take as its value anything from the set of ASCII characters. Character constants are denoted by enclosing the character in single quotes, such as 'h', '%' and '?'. Note that the character constant '6' is not the same as the integer (or real) value 6. If a non-printing character has to be referred to in the text, it will be given a symbol. For example, the Return (or Enter) key character will be denoted by 'CR'.

In standard ASCII the 128 character values are given a definite order. Numbering them from the 0th to the 127th, the ten digits '0' to '9' occur in respective positions 48 to 57, the upper-case letters 'A' to 'Z' are in positions 65 to 90 and the lower-case letters 'a' to 'z' are in positions 97 to 122. The other characters, printing and non-printing, occupy fixed positions in the gaps. The 128-character ASCII table is given in the Appendix to this unit. (The **Character Map** application in the **Accessories** folder of *Windows* shows the characters in each of the fonts available on your computer. These fonts can contain up to 255 characters, although the first 32 are never shown.)

In this course we shall not have cause to concern ourselves too much about how characters are represented internally by the computer and by C++. In embedded systems and some other areas, such matters are important.

Character data often appears as sequences of characters in strings.

ASCII is another acronym: the American Standard Code for Information Interchange. As it has too few characters for many (human) languages, it is becoming obsolete.

Names like 'CR' come from the typewriter world. There, the Return key caused the carriage holding the paper to physically return to the starting position, hence 'carriage return'.

24

Variables of character type are declared in C^{++} using the keyword **char**. The values that a character variable can take are all character values, including non-printing characters.

There are seven operations on characters: assignment and six comparisons. The availability of the comparison operations arises from having established an (ASCII) order on the members of the character set. For example, each expression in the following list has value true, where *Letter* is a character variable with current value 'k'. (You will need the table in the appendix to check this assertion.)

'a' < 'd',   '9' ≤ 'N',   'r' > 'R',   *Letter* > 'L',
'\$' < *Letter*,   '<' < '>',   '@' ≠ 'a'.

Here is the table detailing the operations and the C^{++} representations.

Design stage symbol	Meaning	C^{++} version
character	single character	**char**
←	assignment	=
=	is equal to	==
≠	is not equal to	!=
<	is earlier in ASCII order than	<
>	is later in ASCII order than	>
≤	is earlier than or equal to	<=
≥	is later than or equal to	>=

One final point to mention about characters is that they share with integers the property of being **ordinal** data. What this means, in a nutshell, is that it is data which can be used for counting. For example, given any two integer values, you can count off (or list in order) *all* the integers which lie between them. The same is true of characters. Although you might need to refer to the ASCII character table to do it, you can, for example, list all the characters in order from 'A' to 'g' (of which there are 39). The reals do not constitute an ordinal data type: for example, you cannot list *all* the real numbers which lie between 1.1 and 1.2.

2.5 Strings

Intuitively, a string is a sequence of characters. To distinguish between strings and characters, we use double quotation marks to delimit strings. For example, "MY FIRST STRING" is a string constant consisting of only upper-case characters and space characters. A string constant can be made up of any of the characters, including non-printing ones (although the latter will rarely occur).

Where needed for clarity, the symbol '□' is used to denote a single space character. So the above string might be written as "MY□FIRST□STRING" to highlight the single spaces between words.

The values that a string variable can take are all possible string constants. This is one area where the limitations imposed by the computer's hardware may become very real. In order to accommodate a string of the maximum length allowed by Builder, there has to be over 2 gigabytes of storage available. At the time of writing, this is a common limit on the total storage (RAM and hard disk) provided on a personal compuer. Much of it will not be available for a single variable to use! Unlike the earlier data types, strings are not discussed in detail here. For the time being, all that is needed are string constants. There are a number of very useful operations on strings available, which are discussed in *Unit 3*.

> One reason for wanting to distinguish between strings and characters is that there are operations on strings which do not really make sense for characters.

> Where there is no doubt, the '□' symbol is omitted.

> Actual programming languages inevitably impose some sort of limit on the set of string constants. In the Builder implementation of C++, the limitation is not likely to trouble us since strings exceeding 2 billion characters are permitted!

2.6 Boolean variables

Boolean data items have just two possible values, **true** and **false**. Despite this paucity of possible values, you will discover that boolean variables are very useful in problem solving. In addition, true and false also crop up frequently as values of expressions used in statements, as you have seen in exercises in this section. An expression whose value is either true or false is commonly called a **condition**. You will see that conditions arise naturally in connection with important design constructions that you will encounter in the next section.

There are three operators on the boolean data type. First there are two operators which combine boolean values to give another boolean value. These are the **disjunction** and **conjunction** operators which, in designs, are denoted by **or** and **and** respectively. They are defined as follows.

Let A and B be two boolean values. Then

A **or** B has value $\begin{cases} \text{true, if either } A \text{ or } B \text{ is true (or both),} \\ \text{false, if both } A \text{ and } B \text{ are false;} \end{cases}$

A **and** B has value $\begin{cases} \text{true, if both } A \text{ and } B \text{ are true,} \\ \text{false, if either } A \text{ or } B \text{ is false (or both).} \end{cases}$

> A and B may arise as boolean constants — true or false — as values of boolean variables or as values of conditions.

The third operator, **not** (called **negation**), applies to a single boolean operand and switches its value. That is,

not A has value $\begin{cases} \text{true, if } A \text{ is false,} \\ \text{false, if } A \text{ is true.} \end{cases}$

Thus, if *Cond1* and *Cond2* are boolean variables with current values **true** and **false** respectively, then

Cond1 **or** *Cond2* = true,   *Cond1* **and** *Cond2* = false,
not *Cond1* = false,   **not** *Cond2* = true.

Exercise 2.5 _____

If _Continue_ is a boolean variable with value **true**, and _Count_ is an integer variable with value 10, what are the values of the following boolean conditions?

(a) **not** _Continue_

(b) _Continue_ = **true**

(c) _Continue_ **or** (_Count_ < 6)

(d) (_Count_ ≤ 10) **and** (_Count_ % 3 = 2)

(e) **not** (_Count_ > 0) **or** ('a' < 'h')

(f) **not** (_Continue_ **or** ('a' < 'h'))

[_Solution on page 47_]

The table showing the operations on the boolean data type is given below. Note that the keyword for a boolean variable is **bool**, and that the C^{++} symbols corresponding to design's **or**, **and** and **not** are ‖, && and !, respectively.

Design stage symbol	Meaning	C^{++} version
boolean	boolean	**bool**
←	assignment	=
=	is equal to	==
≠	is not equal to	!=
or	disjunction	‖
and	conjunction	&&
not	negation	!

In the coming units you will see many ways in which boolean variables can be used.

3 Extending the mean problem

The problem discussed in Section 1 (finding the mean of four numbers) is now extended to a problem which is more in need of a computer solution. You will find that the *nature* of the design changes, as well as the details.

3.1 Loops

Having written a program to determine the mean value of four numbers entered from the keyboard, a start has been made on writing a general program to determine the mean of any collection of numbers. In this subsection that original problem is extended and generalised. As the problem becomes more involved, new design constructs must be introduced to help create an algorithm (i.e. method) for the solution. As a first step in that direction, let us suppose that instead of using just four numbers, the mean of 50 numbers is required. Can the solution to the four number problem be modified, or is it back to the drawing board?

The noun *construct* is really an alternative word for *construction*, but tends to be used by computer scientists.

Problem Specification   Mean 2

Write a program to receive 50 whole numbers in the range 0 to 100 inclusive entered at the keyboard, and to write out their mean value.   □

The numbers concerned might be percentages, such as the overall scores of fifty MT262 students on an assignment.

In one sense the problem has not really changed and the same algorithm could be used: read in the 50 numbers, store them in 50 variables, add them up, divide by 50 to determine the mean, and finally write out the mean. However, the use of 50 variables and the cumbersome nature of the calculation of the mean should force a rethink of the whole approach.

Forget for a moment the fact that a machine is being used and suppose that you are given the task of working out this mean. You are going to be given 50 numbers, one at a time, and you are asked to determine the mean value. What will you do? You might write all the 50 numbers on paper. Then again, perhaps you would not. There is no need to remember the numbers. Why not just add them as they are given to you, and divide the final total by 50?

"Can you do addition?" the White Queen asked. "What's one and one and one and one and one and one and one and one and one and one and one?"
"I don't know," said Alice, "I lost count." — *Through the Looking-Glass*, Lewis Carroll.

Applying this in the machine context means that there is no need to store all the given numbers using 50 variables; you could add them up as they are entered. That is, you can imagine repeating 50 times the activity of reading a number entered from the keyboard and adding it to a running total. The repetition can be illustrated as follows.

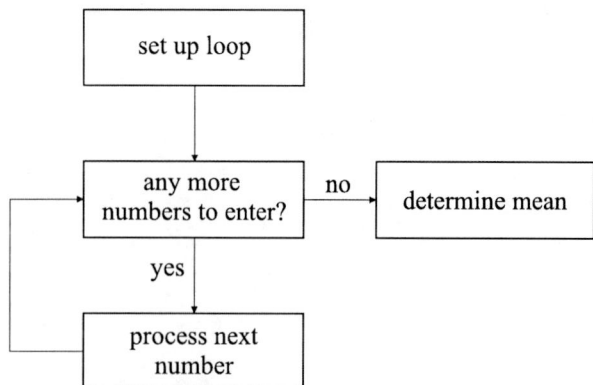

The individual instructions given to a machine in a computer program only ask that it perform very simple tasks. The power of the computer resides in its ability to carry out each instruction very quickly and, consequently, being able to carry out large numbers of instructions in a short time. The program itself should not contain a very large number of instructions or it would take an age for the program to be designed, never mind keyed into the machine. The answer to this dilemma lies in the fact that designs of computer programs capitalise on the ability to repeat sequences of steps over and over again. Such repeated sequences are referred to as **loops**. The above diagram amply illustrates a loop: execution goes round and round, processing numbers until all the numbers have been entered. Although the processing occurs 50 times, setting up the loop to make it happen should require only a few instructions.

The above diagram leads to this top-level design for the revised problem.

At top level, the aim is to capture the overall structure of the solution without going into detail.

1   set up loop
2   **loop** while there are more numbers to enter
3   process next number
4   **loopend**
5   determine mean value

(This does not quite fit the 'input–process–output' format observed earlier. The input and process steps are interleaved.)

Look at the chosen design style in steps 2–4. The word **loop** in step 2 starts the loop, and **loopend** marks the finish. Between these two, indented, comes the **loop body**. This is the sequence of instructions which is to be repeated. At the moment there is just one step in the loop body, but the number of steps will increase as the design is refined. Finally, note that the opening loop step includes the condition governing continued repetition. At the moment this is the somewhat woolly 'while there are more numbers to enter'; just what this is to entail will have to be clarified as the design is refined.

How is this loop going to be controlled? It is to be repeated exactly 50 times. After the 50th number is processed, execution must move on to step 5. The way to make this happen is to count the numbers as they are entered. Initially, the count will have value 0, because no numbers have been entered, and it will be increased by 1 each time a number is processed. The loop is exited when the count has reached 50. Our earlier figure can be modified to highlight the use of the count, as follows.

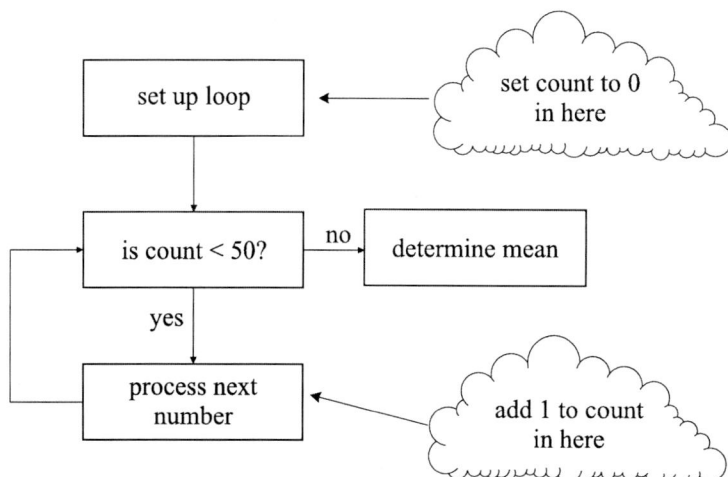

This discussion has identified one variable of our program. An integer variable — call it *Count* — is needed for counting the numbers as they are entered from the keyboard. What other variables are going to appear in the solution?

Exercise 3.1

Draw up a provisional data table for this design.

[*Solution on page 47*]

Step 1 was included in the design as a 'catch-all'. Invariably, when a loop is used in a design, one or more variables used in the loop have to be **initialised**. Initialising a variable means assigning to it a starting value. Here the variable *Count*, used to count the entered numbers, must be initialised to 0 before counting starts.

Exercise 3.2

Of the three other variables identified in the solution for Exercise 3.1, which require initialisation before the loop?

[*Solution on page 47*]

Enough progress has been made for a first refinement of our design to be written out. This refinement recognises that the processing, in step 3, will split into three tasks: reading in the next number, adding this number to the total, and incrementing by 1 the count of numbers.

1.1   *Count* ← 0
1.2   *Total* ← 0
2.1   **loop** while *Count* < 50
3.1   read in *NextNumber*
3.2   add *NextNumber* to *Total*
3.3   add 1 to *Count*
4   **loopend**
5.1   calculate *Mean*
5.2   write out *Mean*

> Step 2.1 is just the refinement of step 2 expressed in terms of *Count*.

Steps 3.1 and 5.2 will refine just as the corresponding ones did in the first version of the problem, and steps 3.2 and 3.3 require no more than conversion into the correct form for assignment statements. The calculation in step 5.1 is not quite as it was before, but should not be too difficult for you to deal with.

Exercise 3.3

Refine the design above to a final design.

[*Solution on page 48*]

You are not asked to code, and test, the solution now. First, you are asked to investigate a further extension to the problem.

3.2 Selection

The progression from finding the mean of four numbers to finding the mean of 50 numbers led to a very different solution that made use of a loop. There is nothing special about the 50 here; the program can be readily adapted to determine the mean value of any collection of whole numbers, provided we know how many numbers there are. We have to do nothing more than change the '50' in the loop condition to the revised number and, later, divide by this new number (instead of 50) in the calculation of *Mean*. But suppose that we do not know in advance how many numbers are going to be given for averaging.

Problem Specification   Mean 3

A collection of whole numbers in the range from 0 to 100 inclusive is to be provided. Write a program whose purpose is to receive these numbers entered at the keyboard, and to write out their mean value.   □

The same top-level design as before will suffice for solution to this revised problem; numbers are entered from the keyboard in a controlled loop, and when all have been entered, the mean value is determined and written out.

1   set up loop
2   **loop** while there are more numbers to enter
3   process next number
4   **loopend**
5   determine mean value

As refinement takes place, the one new aspect to be sorted out concerns how the loop is to be controlled. One can imagine the numbers being supplied on paper with the user keying them in one after the other. The user will know when the last one has been entered, but how can that information be conveyed to the machine? One way is to make use of what is called a **sentinel** value, a marker to indicate that input is finished. Some value which is not possible as a genuine entry is chosen as a sentinel. When the sentinel is entered in response to the prompt for another number, it is to be interpreted as a signal that the end of the list has been reached.

For this problem the numbers being entered lie in the range from 0 to 100 inclusive. So, for example, -1 can be used as a sentinel with the following loop control step.

2.1   **loop** while $NextNumber \neq -1$

This will force exit from the loop when -1 is read in response to the prompt in step 3.

Any value not in the range 0 to 100 may be used as a sentinel. It must be of the same type as valid entries, because it will be entered when a number is expected.

The following is an attempt at a first refinement incorporating the sentinel to control the loop. All that has been done is to take the solution to the previous version of the problem and change the loop control (step 2.1) and the calculation of *Mean* (step 5.1.1).

1.1 $Count \leftarrow 0$

1.2 $Total \leftarrow 0$

2.1   **loop** while $NextNumber \neq -1$

3.1.1   write out "Enter next number: "

3.1.2   read in *NextNumber*

3.2.1 $Total \leftarrow Total + NextNumber$

3.3.1 $Count \leftarrow Count + 1$

4   **loopend**

5.1.1 $Mean \leftarrow Total/Count$

5.2.1 write out "The mean value is "

5.2.2 write out *Mean*

Exercise 3.4

There are two flaws in this design, each is to do with the use of a sentinel. Can you spot what they are?

(Do not spend too long on this before checking the solution.)

[*Solution on page 48*]

As explained in the solution to Exercise 3.4, the problem with the loop body is that when -1 is entered, steps 3.2.1 and 3.3.1 need to be by-passed. There is a design construct for this: the **if** step. It enables the design of steps 3.2.1 and 3.3.1 to be reconsidered, along the following lines.

3.2.1   **if** $NextNumber \neq -1$ **then**

3.2.2 $Total \leftarrow Total + NextNumber$

3.2.3 $Count \leftarrow Count + 1$

3.2.4   **else**

3.2.5   do nothing

3.2.6   **ifend**

This is not a refinement of the above design; it is a redesign. Hence the numbering is started again.

The **if** step is an example of what is called a **selection**, and introduces **branching** in the program: select either one sequence of instructions to follow, or another. Its general format is

> **if** condition **then**
>   steps for **then** branch
> **else**
>   steps for **else** branch
> **ifend**
> next step follows both branches

Depending on whether the condition is true or false, the steps in the **then** branch or the steps in the **else** branch give the sequence of instructions to be carried out. The number of steps in each of these branches could be very large or, as in the case of the **else** branch in our present program, the branch might contain no steps at all. (This latter situation is represented in the design by adding the single 'phoney' step *do nothing*.) The **ifend** step signals the point at which the two branches come together again.

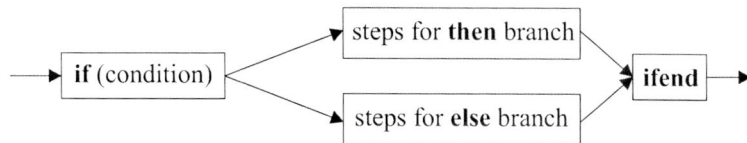

Exercise 3.5

Consider the following design, in which an integer variable *Number* is involved. The design involves two **if** steps, one within the other, as indicated by the layout.

```
1    if Number is greater than 6 then
2        Number ← Number − 2
3    else
4        if Number is less than 2 then
5            Number ← Number + 2
6        else
7            write out Number
8        ifend
9    ifend
```

Trace the path through this design if the value of *Number* on entry is

(a) 0,

(b) 4,

(c) 10.

In each case, indicate the resulting value of *Number*.

[*Solution on page 48*]

There is one final, important, point to make regarding the solution of the third version of the mean problem. It is all well and good having input terminated by entry of a sentinel value, but the user of the program must know about it. If a user of our program does not know that the end of input is to be indicated by entering -1, then that person is hardly likely to discover this fact accidentally! The moral is that the program must contain a prompt explaining how to terminate input. This is included as part of the prompt for input in the following final design.

1.1 $Count \leftarrow 0$
1.2 $Total \leftarrow 0$
1.3 $NextNumber \leftarrow 0$
2.1   **loop** while $NextNumber \neq -1$
3.1.1   write out "Enter next number or -1 to stop: "
3.1.2   read in $NextNumber$
3.2.1   **if** $NextNumber \neq -1$ **then**
3.2.2 $Total \leftarrow Total + NextNumber$
3.2.3 $Count \leftarrow Count + 1$
3.2.4   **else**
3.2.5   do nothing
3.2.6   **ifend**
4   **loopend**
5.1.1 $Mean \leftarrow Total/Count$
5.2.1 write out "The mean value is "
5.2.2 write out $Mean$

The majority of the individual steps in this design are assignment statements, read in statements or write out statements, all of which you have seen how to code. To carry through the coding of this design, it remains to explain how to code the loop and the selection. These coding ideas are introduced in the next section.

4 Coding loops and selection

To complete the coding of the solution of the Mean 3 problem requires both a loop and a selection. C++ provides a number of different loop and selection constructs; only those needed for the current problem are introduced here.

4.1 Coding an if step

The general form of the code for an **if** step is called an **if** statement. In C++ it is as follows.

The general format of an **if** step (in design) is given on page 32.

```
if (condition)
{
  statement 1;
  statement 2;
  ... ;
}
else
{
  statement 1;
  statement 2;
  ... ;
}
```

Note the following features of this construct.

o The word **then** used in design does not appear in the C++ coded version.

o The condition (which is always held in brackets) can be *any* expression that yields a boolean value.

o The **then** actions and the **else** actions are each delimited by a pair of braces (curly brackets) within which there is a sequence of C++ statements. These sequences of statements are called the **then clause** and the **else clause**, respectively. The braces are essential if there is more than one statement in the **then** clause or in the **else** clause, but may be omitted if there is a single statement. There must *not* be a semicolon after the closing brace of a **then** clause or an **else** clause.

o The layout of the statement is course style, and you are expected to adopt it. The spacing and line breaks are of no consequence to the compiler, but help with the readability of the code.

The following remarks concern a special case and introduce a definition.

o For many **if** steps, the **else** action is 'do nothing'. For this special case, in the code the keyword **else** and its clause are usually omitted.

o A sequence of two or more statements is called a **compound statement**.

o A compound statement is always held together by braces, and the closing brace is *not* followed by a semicolon.

The best way to come to terms with the **if** statement is to witness some examples.

Exercise 4.1 —————————————————————————————

Study the following code, in which *Next* is an integer variable, and then answer the questions about it.

```
if (Next % 2 == 1)
 Next = 3 * Next - 1;
else
{
  Next = Next/2;
  WriteInt(Next);
}
```

(a) Identify the **then** clause and the **else** clause in this **if** statement. Are either of these compound statements?

(b) Explain the presence of the one pair of braces in this code.

(c) What happens if this code is executed when, initially, *Next* has the value 14?

[Solution on page 49]

—————————————————————————————

The next example is more complex: this time, one **if** statement is nested within another. (You saw the design version of such a situation in Exercise 3.5.) In what follows, *Grade* is a character variable and all other variables are of integer type. Note carefully that when entering a character value in code, the value is enclosed by two right quote marks.

```
if (Age > 16)
{
  Majority = Majority + 1;
  if (Grade == 'A')
    Target = Target + 1;
}
else
  Target = Target - 1;
```

The outer **if** statement has the following structure.

```
if (condition)
 {compound statement}
else
 single statement;
```

It looks complex because the compound statement which forms the **then** clause comprises two statements, the second of which is another **if** statement. This 'inner' **if** statement has no **else** clause associated with it; there is an implicit '**else** do nothing'.

To check that you follow all the branching in this code, try the following exercise.

This example highlights the importance of the **ifend** steps in our design. They leave no ambiguity concerning where an **if** step ends.

Exercise 4.2

Determine the results of executing the complete given **if** statement when, on entry, *Majority* has value 237, *Target* has value 8, and:

(a) *Age* has value 16 and *Grade* has value 'A';

(b) *Age* has value 17 and *Grade* has value 'A';

(c) *Age* has value 18 and *Grade* has value 'B'.

[Solution on page 49]

Nested **if**s are looked at more closely in the next unit; for now you will be concerned only with not-too-complicated **if**s. The next exercise asks you to write, rather than read, code that involves **if**.

It is often convenient, as here, to refer to '**if**s' rather than '**if** constructs'.

Exercise 4.3

Write the C^{++} code for the following design fragment for some program. In the design, *Ch* and *Wanted* are character variables, *Found* is a boolean variable and *Count* and *Failures* are integer variables. You need not include their declarations.

```
1     if Ch = Wanted then
2.1       Found ← true
2.2       Count ← Count + 1
3     else
4.1       Found ← false
4.2       Failures ← Failures + 1
5     ifend
```

[Solution on page 49]

4.2 Coding a while loop

The general form of the code for a **while** loop is called a **while** statement.
In C^{++} it is as follows.

```
while (condition)
  {single or compound statement}
```

The condition (which is held in brackets) can be any expression giving a
boolean result (that is, **true** or **false**), and the loop body codes as a single
or compound statement. As with the **then** and **else** clauses, if the loop
body comprises a single (non-compound) statement, then the braces may
be omitted.

Remember: a compound
statement is a sequence of
C^{++} statements held in
braces, and does *not* have a
semicolon after the closing
brace.

Here are a couple of examples of code fragments using loops. The first
involves two integer variables, *Next* and *Target*, which you may assume
have been declared. Try to work out what the fragment is achieving before
reading the commentary that follows.

```
Target = ReadIntPr("Enter target: ");
Next = 1;
while (Next * Next < Target)
    Next = Next + 1;
WriteInt(Next);
```

The loop body in this code comprises a *single* statement, which increments
Next; hence braces are not needed to enclose the loop body. Notice how
indentation has been used to highlight this feature; the loop body will
always be indented.

This code can be paraphrased as follows. A target number is read in from
the keyboard. The variable *Next* is set to 1 and repeatedly increased by
one until the condition *Next * Next < Target* is false. The final value of
Next is written out. In summary, the smallest positive integer whose square
exceeds the entered target (no matter whether *Target* is positive, zero or
negative) is determined and written out.

The second example includes an **if** statement in the loop body. Read the
code, and then answer the questions about it in the following exercise. In
this code *Ch* is a variable of type **char**.

```
Ch = '*';
while (Ch != 'A')
{
 Ch = ReadCharPr("Enter your guess: ");
 if (Ch == 'a')
    WriteString("Try Capitals!");
}
```

Exercise 4.4

(a) Identify the loop body.

(b) How is the loop halted?

(c) What is the purpose of the statement preceding the loop?

[*Solution on page 50*]

4.3 Coding the revised solution

You should now have enough experience of **while** and **if** to tackle the task of coding the final design reached at the end of Section 3 for the revised mean problem. As always at this stage of development, you are strongly advised to write down the code for your design, using pencil and paper, before going to the computer. Hence the coding task is set as an exercise first, and you can check your answer against the one given in the solution before proceeding to the practical activity stage of keying in your code.

Exercise 4.5 _____

Write C++ code for the final design for the mean problem.

[*Solution on page 50*]

The next move is to test *your* coding.

Computer Activity 4.1 _____

Start Builder and open a new console application.

    File|New...|Console Wizard

See Computer Activity 1.1 for the full instructions for opening a new console application.

Use File|Save Project As... to save the project in the Block I subfolder of MT262. Use the names Mean2U for the unit file and Mean2 for the project file.

As you have done before, make the MT262 course library available by using Project|Add to Project... to add MT262io.lib.

Then add the following statement.

```
#include "MT262io.h"
```

Also, to hold the screen output, add the statement

```
getchar();
```

just above the **return 0;** statement.

Now carefully type in your solution to Exercise 4.5.

After correcting any errors that emerge at compilation, run your program several times using various collections of numbers to test that it functions as intended. (Because of poor error handling, do not make −1 the first entry. You should be careful to enter only integers. A discussion of these points is given in *Unit 4*.)

[*Solution on page 53*]

If you make an error and your program goes into an infinite loop press **Ctrl+C** and click **OK** in the resulting dialog box. You will not lose any of your work in Builder.

You have now carried through the coding of a fairly reasonable program to calculate the means of numbers entered from the keyboard. Errors are still not handled well, as zeros arising from faulty data entry (reals or characters being entered) cannot be distinguished from 'genuine' zeros. Such matters really should be dealt with by refining the 'read in *NextNumber*' step to validate that the user has entered what was intended. The example has served its purpose by introducing you to the top-down approach to design, refinement of designs and the coding of **while** loops and **if** steps. In the next section you are invited to design and code a solution to a similar type of problem.

5 A worked example

In this final section you are invited to work right through an example, from problem specification to C++ program. The intention is that you do so with guidance, but if you feel confident enough to tackle the problem entirely on your own, then by all means do so. It must be emphasised, however, that design of computer programs is an art and there is no such thing as *the* solution to a problem. It is most unlikely that, if you choose to go off on your own, you will reach the same solution to this problem as the course team. Indeed, there may well be solutions more elegant than that designed by the course team.

This example is intended to review the key concepts that you have encountered in this unit. No new ideas will be introduced.

This is the challenge.

Problem Specification   Coin Tossing

A statistician wishes to carry out an experiment involving tossing a coin. Let 'heads' be denoted by 'H' and 'tails' by 'T'. If tossing a coin 20 times gives

  T T T T H H T H H H H H H H T H T T T T T

then this comprises a number of sequences of equal outcomes:

  4T, then 2H, then 1T, then 6H, then 1T, then 1H, and finally 5T.

There are 7 sequences in all, and the figure

$$(4 + 2 + 1 + 6 + 1 + 1 + 5)/7 = 20/7 = 2.857$$

represents the mean of their lengths. Note that the sum of the lengths of the sequences is equal to the number of tosses.

The statistician is interested in this mean figure and anticipates repeating the experiment many times using numbers of tosses greater than 20.

Your task is to design and code a C++ program to help the statistician (the user) analyse the experiment. For each toss of the coin, the statistician is to enter either 'H' or 'T' at the keyboard. At some time of the statistician's choosing, the experiment can be halted, at which point the required mean is to be written to the screen.   □

Is the problem clearly specified? The specification has left one or two grey areas, such as how the experiment is to be stopped, but it should be possible to make some design decisions which resolve these matters to the satisfaction of the user.

Where should you start? First a top-level design is needed. This should try to capture the overall structure of a program without going into any detail, and involves thinking about how 'input–process–output' is to be handled. You can probably envisage that results of tosses (represented by characters 'H' or 'T') are entered in a loop which the user can cause to halt. As each character is entered, it is processed in some way. When input finishes, the results of this processing have to be processed and the required mean written out.

The processing involved may still not be clear, but do not worry about that yet.

That description should be sufficient to write down a top-level design.

Exercise 5.1 _____

Write down a top-level design for a solution to this problem.

[Solution on page 50]

The top-level design has broken down the problem into a number of subtasks, and any one can be picked up next. The suggestion is that you begin with the loop control. The decision that the user will enter 'H' (for heads) or 'T' (for tails) on each pass of the loop seems perfectly sensible. One way of controlling the loop is to allow the user to enter a *sentinel value* instead. 'Q' (for quit) is a reasonable choice for such a sentinel value.

Exercise 5.2 _____

Refine the loop control step 2. In doing so, you should introduce one variable which the program is going to employ.

Exercise 5.3 _____

Think about what other variables are going to be needed and draw up a provisional data table.

[Solutions on page 51]

You are now asked to look at the processing in step 3. Since, in the loop body, just one character is read in and processed, step 3 can be refined as follows.

3.1   read in *Toss*

3.2   process this input

Consider step 3.2. 'H', 'T' or 'Q' has just been entered and requires processing. This will cause a branch: different actions are needed depending on which value is entered. Handling the 'Q' entry should be straightforward. When 'Q' is entered, there is nothing to be done other than let the loop control stop the loop and go on to the calculation of the mean. On the other hand, if either 'H' or 'T' is entered, then one more must be added to the count of tosses and .... Let us not try to do too much analysis all at once. We have made progress in recognising how step 3.2 is beginning to refine, so let us record it.

Do not concern yourself with erroneous entries being made by the user.

3.1   read in *Toss*

3.2.1 **if** *Toss* ≠ 'Q' **then**

3.2.2   *Total* ← *Total* + 1

3.2.3   process 'H' or 'T'

3.2.4 **else**

3.2.5   do nothing

3.2.6 **ifend**

Attention can now move on to step 3.2.3. The processing here is not going to be so much concerned with whether the present toss is 'H' or 'T' but rather with whether or not it switches from the previous value. For example, if the previous toss was 'H' (so that a sequence of 'H' values is currently being processed), then a toss of 'H' continues the present sequence whereas a toss of 'T' means another sequence is started. A refinement of step 3.2.3 can be based on the following sequence of steps.

```
    if Toss is not the same as previous toss then
        process end of sequence
    else
        process continuation of sequence
    ifend
```

Your next task is to finalise the design of step 3. To do so, another variable will be needed. In order to count the number of sequences, a switch between 'H' and 'T' must be noted, and one way to do this is to keep a record of the previous toss.

Exercise 5.4 _____

Finalise the design of step 3. Your steps should use the variables of a revised data table, and each step should be ready for coding.

[*Solution on page 51*]

The design is almost complete. Refinement of step 5, the calculation and writing out of *Mean*, is something that has been done before. All that remains is to decide which variables need to be initialised, and to what values.

Exercise 5.5 _____

Write out a final design for this solution.

[*Solution on page 52*]

Finally, you are asked to code and run your program. As always, you should plan the practical activity fully, writing your code out on paper, before venturing to the keyboard.

Computer Activity 5.1 _____

To run your coded design, follow the sequence of activities given below. These are given in a fairly brief form, so you should refer to practical activities from earlier sections if you need further guidance.

o   Start Builder and open a new console application.
o   Save the project using the names `StatsU` for the unit file and `Stats` for the project file.
o   Add `MT262io.lib` to the project.
o   In the Code Editor window, enter the `#include "MT262io.h"` statement.
o   Add the statement required to hold the screen output.
o   Carefully enter your coded solution to the problem.
o   Attempt to run the program. Correct any errors which are reported.
o   When the program is running successfully, test it by entering suitable data. (Because of poor error handling, do not make 'Q' the first entry. The errors that occur if you do will be discussed in *Unit 4*.)

If you fail to get your program running, you can inspect the course team version by opening the project `CTStats.bpr` and running it.

[*Solution on page 53*]

Objectives

After studying this unit, you should be able to:

o provide a top-level design for a solution to a simple non-trivial problem;

o refine a design step making use of

    – **if**...**then**...**else**...**ifend**,

    – **while** loops,

    – sentinel values;

o refine a design until it is ready for coding, in particular by making appropriate variable declarations and initialising relevant variables;

o use the standard numbering system for design steps, through all stages;

o translate a final design into C^{++} code;

o use recommended spacing, indentation and line breaks when writing designs and code;

o use the standard design and C^{++} symbols given in the tables on pages 21, 24, 25 and 27;

o use and understand the use of the following terms: top-level design, final design, coding, keyword, variable, assignment of variables, declaration of variables, variable type, data table, identifier, function, if step, if statement, then clause, else clause, branching, while loop, loop body, condition, negation, conjunction, disjunction, floating point representation of numbers.

Appendix: The ASCII table

The following table shows the standard (128-character) ASCII table. Only a few of the non-printing characters are named; the others are of no use in this course. The characters are not enclosed in quotes.

Number	Character	Number	Character	Number	Character	Number	Character
0		32	space	64	@	96	
1		33	!	65	A	97	a
2		34	"	66	B	98	b
3		35	#	67	C	99	c
4		36	$	68	D	100	d
5		37	%	69	E	101	e
6		38	&	70	F	102	f
7		39	'	71	G	103	g
8		40	(	72	H	104	h
9	'TAB'	41	)	73	I	105	i
10	'LF'	42	*	74	J	106	j
11		43	+	75	K	107	k
12		44	,	76	L	108	l
13	'CR'	45	–	77	M	109	m
14		46	.	78	N	110	n
15		47	/	79	O	111	o
16		48	0	80	P	112	p
17		49	1	81	Q	113	q
18		50	2	82	R	114	r
19		51	3	83	S	115	s
20		52	4	84	T	116	t
21		53	5	85	U	117	u
22		54	6	86	V	118	v
23		55	7	87	W	119	w
24		56	8	88	X	120	x
25		57	9	89	Y	121	y
26	'EOF'	58	:	90	Z	122	z
27	'ESC'	59	;	91	[	123	{
28		60	<	92	\	124	|
29		61	=	93	]	125	}
30		62	>	94	^	126	~
31		63	?	95	–	127	delete

Note that 'LF' stands for 'line feed', i.e. produce a new line, 'ESC' for 'escape' and 'CR' for 'carriage return'. Character number 96 is not defined in ASCII but is used for a variety of characters; for example, it is often used for the single left quote and for the British pound symbol.

Solutions to the Exercises

Section 1

Solution 1.1
Dividing an integer total by 4 may well give a decimal part in the result, so the mean of four whole numbers will, in general, be a real number. For this problem, the specification might be that the answer is to be a real number given to two decimal places.

Solution 1.2
Before anything is done with the four numbers read in at step 1, they have to be stored. So four variables, each of which is to hold integer values, are needed. *First, Second, Third* and *Fourth* seem like appropriate identifiers for them. You may well have chosen different names for variables having the same descriptions as those given.

In step 2 the mean value is calculated, and a variable will probably be needed for storing the answer. A suitable identifier is *Mean*, and it will be a real variable because the mean of four whole numbers will, in general, not be a whole number.

That is five variables. You might have thought of others. For example, if you decided you would need a variable *Total* to hold the sum of the four input numbers, then you are thinking on sound lines. But, as you will see, that variable can probably be avoided.

Solution 1.3
The refinement is

3.1   write out *Mean*

There are three things to note.
○   As this is a refinement of step 3, the numbering begins at 3.1, and as there is only one step in the refinement, it ends there.
○   You had not been given the design step for writing out but, by analogy with reading in (in step 1), you could probably guess this.
○   The actual identifier, *Mean*, is used in the design step rather than the descriptive expression 'the mean value'.

Solution 1.4
The step becomes

2.1   *Mean* ← (*First* + *Second* + *Third* + *Fourth*)/4

Solution 1.5
This declares *Mean* to be a real variable. You might therefore conclude that, in the same way as **int** is used to identify integer type, **float** is the word used for 'real type'. Real variables and the use of **float** are discussed in the next section.

Solution 1.6

(a) *MyInt* and *YourInt* are declared to be integer variables.

(b) An integer value is read in from the keyboard in response to the prompt "Enter any whole number: ", and this value is assigned to *YourInt*.

(c) The value assigned to *MyInt* is obtained by adding 6 to the current value of *YourInt*; that is, to the value read in from the keyboard. No wonder the machine's number is always bigger!

You probably worked out what *WriteString* does. It writes to the monitor screen the string value in the accompanying brackets. In this case the value is the string constant " ... my number is bigger so I win again!".

Section 2

Solution 2.1

gross%, *#pounds* and *my*program* are not allowed as each contains an illegal symbol. All the others are acceptable identifiers. (Note that *x_0* and *a_to_z* are legal, but would not be used in this course.)

Solution 2.2

(a) 36

(b) −72

(c) 60

(d) In Builder's implementation of C++, this evaluates to −60. However, it should not really be regarded as a legal expression (see the fuller comment below).

Brackets are really needed to distinguish the expression in (c) from that in (b). The brackets determine the order in which calculations are carried out in compound expressions. Without brackets, the order of calculation is governed by a precedence of the operations. Multiplication (and division) take precedence over addition and subtraction so, in (b), the expression 7 * *Total* is evaluated first, and then this becomes the second operand in the remaining subtraction. In (d) the minus sign denotes a negative number and *not* subtraction; taking the negative of a number has precedence (in C++) over multiplication.

Solution 2.3

(a) False.

(b) True. The remainder on dividing 9 by 4 is 1. Hence 9 % 4 = 1, and the comparison 1 ≥ 1 has value true.

(c) False. The two sides do have the same integer value, namely 12.

(d) True.

Note that the expressions on the left in (b), (c) and (d) do not need brackets. Where comparison operators are involved, the operands to left and right are evaluated fully before the comparison is attempted. It may, however, still be a good idea to include extra brackets to make the meaning quite clear. Thus it might be wise to write (3 * 4) ≠ *Total*, even though the brackets are not essential.

Solution 2.4

(a) −5.42

(b) 1.855

(c) True. The expression on the right does not require brackets, but (2 * *First*) would be clearer.

Solution 2.5

(a) False, as *Continue* has value true.

(b) True. But notice that the '= true' is redundant in the following sense. Whatever the value of *Continue*, true or false, the expression *Continue* = true has the same value as *Continue*.

(c) True. *Continue* has value true and (*Count* < 6) has value false, so the disjunction has value true.

(d) False. As *Count* % 3 has value 1, the condition on the right is false, and so the conjunction is false.

(e) True. This is the disjunction of two conditions, the right-hand one of which is true.

(f) False. This is the negation of a disjunction. The disjunction has value true — in fact, both conditions involved are true — so the negation is false.

Section 3

Solution 3.1

The design developed after this exercise involves the variables in the following data table. Even if your descriptions match those given, you may well have chosen different identifiers.

Type	Identifier	Description
Integer	*Count*	Count of numbers entered
Integer	*NextNumber*	Number read from the keyboard
Integer	*Total*	Total of numbers entered so far
Real	*Mean*	The required mean value

Solution 3.2

The variable *Total* must be initialised to 0. It is summing the numbers entered, and so the sum must be set to 0 before the first number is read in.

The value of *NextNumber* will be read from the keyboard. It does not require initialisation, as any value prior to the first one read in is of no consequence.

The variable *Mean* is calculated after the loop. There is no reason to give it some artificial value beforehand.

Solution 3.3

1.1 $Count \leftarrow 0$

1.2 $Total \leftarrow 0$

2.1   **loop** while $Count < 50$

3.1.1   write out "Enter next number: "

3.1.2   read in $NextNumber$

3.2.1 $Total \leftarrow Total + NextNumber$

3.3.1 $Count \leftarrow Count + 1$

4   **loopend**

5.1.1 $Mean \leftarrow Total/50$

5.2.1 write out "The mean value is "

5.2.2 write out $Mean$

(Did you remember to indent the loop body?)

Solution 3.4

1. When the loop control at step 2.1 is encountered for the first time, the value of $NextNumber$ is checked to see if it is -1 or not. But $NextNumber$ does not have a value yet! For this design, $NextNumber$ must be initialised, prior to the loop, as part of step 1. A suitable initialisation is $NextNumber \leftarrow 0$. The initial value can be any whole number except -1, thereby ensuring that the loop is entered for the first time.

2. As the design stands, if the sentinel value (-1) is entered at step 3.1.2, it is processed. That is, -1 is added to $Total$ and 1 is added to $Count$ (at steps 3.2.1 and 3.3.1) before the loop control moves execution on to step 5.1.1. This, of course, should not happen.

Solution 3.5

(a) When $Number$ has value 0, the condition in step 1 is false, so it is the **else** branch at step 3 which is followed. Now the condition in step 4 is true, so the **then** branch (step 5) is followed. The value of $Number$ is increased by 2 (to 2).

(b) When $Number$ has value 4, the condition in step 1 is again false, so it is the **else** branch at step 3 which is followed. This time the condition at step 4 is false, resulting in the value, 4, being written out as step 7 is carried out.

(c) When $Number$ has value 10, the condition in step 1 is true, so the **then** branch, step 2 alone, is carried out. As a result of this, $Number$ is assigned the value 8.

Section 4

Solution 4.1

(a) The **then** clause comprises the single statement

```
Next = 3 * Next - 1;
```

The **else** clause is the compound statement

```
{
  Next = Next/2;
  WriteInt(Next);
}
```

(b) The **then** clause consists of a single statement and, not being compound, does not require holding braces. The **else** clause is compound, so braces are essential.

(c) When *Next* has value 14, the condition (*Next* % 2 = 1) is false — the remainder on dividing 14 by 2 is 0, which is not equal to 1. Thus the **else** clause is executed. As a result, *Next* is halved to value 7, and this value is written to the screen.

Solution 4.2

(a) As the condition (*Age* > 16) is false, the **else** clause (associated with this outer **if**) is executed. This results in *Target* being decreased in value by 1 to 7.

(b) This time the *Age* condition is true, so the compound **then** clause is executed. The first statement increases *Majority* by 1, and then comes the inner **if**. As the condition (*Grade* = 'A') is true, *Target* is increased by 1. Overall, *Majority* has been increased to 238 and *Target* has been increased to 9.

(c) Again it is the compound **then** clause which is executed. Thus *Majority* is increased by 1 (to 238), but this time the condition (*Grade* = 'A') is false and so no further action is taken. Overall, the only change is the increase of *Majority* to 238. (Neither of the statements involving *Target* is executed.)

Solution 4.3

In checking your answer, make sure that you have included one pair of (round) brackets and two pairs of braces, as all three pairs are essential. Check you have used four semicolons, and that they are in the right places. Check also that you have not confused the symbols '=' and '=='; this is a common source of error. Another thing to check is that you have followed course style in respect of spacing and line breaks.

```
if (Ch == Wanted)
{
  Found = true;
  Count = Count + 1;
}
else
{
  Found = false;
  Failures = Failures + 1;
}
```

Solution 4.4

(a) The loop body, enclosed in the pair of braces, contains two statements. The first statement, which reads a value for *Ch* from the keyboard, is followed by an **if** statement.

(b) The loop is controlled by the condition (*Ch* != 'A'). The loop will halt when the character 'A' is entered from the keyboard in response to the prompt.

Remember that '!=' is the C++ symbol for 'is not equal to'.

(c) This statement initialises the variable *Ch*. This is necessary because the loop condition is tested for the first time before a value of *Ch* has been read from the keyboard, and *Ch* must already have a value at this time. (Any character other than 'A' could replace '*'.)

Solution 4.5

```
int Count;
int Total;
int NextNumber;
float Mean;
 Count = 0;
 Total = 0;
 NextNumber = 0;
 while (NextNumber != -1)
 {
   NextNumber = ReadIntPr("Enter next number or -1 to stop: ");
   if (NextNumber != -1)
   {
     Total = Total + NextNumber;
     Count = Count + 1;
   }
 }
 Mean = float(Total)/Count;
 WriteFloatPr("The mean value is ", Mean);
```

Section 5

Solution 5.1

One top-level design is as follows.

1   initialise variables
2   **loop** while more tosses to come
3   process next toss
4   **loopend**
5   write out results

Following the earlier example, you might have written step 1 as *set up loop*. What setting up the loop entails is making sure that variables used in the loop are all initialised if necessary. Henceforth the 'catch-all' step *initialise variables* will be used. (This top-level design is the basis for a general top-level design for solutions which involve looping.)

Solution 5.2

2.1   **loop** while *Toss* ≠ 'Q'

Here the character variable *Toss* has been used to hold the value of the most recent keyboard input ('H', 'T' or 'Q').

Solution 5.3

The processing involves counting the total number of tosses and the number of sequences of equal outcomes, so integer counting variables for each of these purposes are needed. Perhaps more variables will be needed, but they should become apparent as steps are refined. A provisional data table is as follows.

Type	Identifier	Description
Character	*Toss*	Value of the most recent user entry
Integer	*Total*	Count of total number of tosses
Integer	*SeqCount*	Count of number of sequences of equal outcomes
Real	*Mean*	The mean sequence length

Solution 5.4

The data table above has to be supplemented by a character variable which records the value of the previous toss.

Type	Identifier	Description
Character	*PreviousToss*	Value of previous toss of the coin

When *Toss* is equal to *PreviousToss*, so that the present sequence continues, there is nothing to be done. The toss has already been counted in *Total*, so we continue with the next input. On the other hand, when *Toss* and *PreviousToss* are not equal, the present sequence has ended and the next one started. The tasks then are to increment *SeqCount* and to record the changed value of *PreviousToss*. Putting everything together, and not forgetting that when input is wanted the user needs a prompt, the following design for step 3 is obtained.

3.1.1   write out "Enter H, T (or Q to quit): "
3.1.2   read in *Toss*
3.2.1   **if** *Toss* ≠ 'Q' **then**
3.2.2   *Total* ← *Total* + 1
3.2.3.1   **if** *Toss* ≠ *PreviousToss* **then**
3.2.3.2   *SeqCount* ← *SeqCount* + 1
3.2.3.3   *PreviousToss* ← *Toss*
3.2.3.4   **else**
3.2.3.5   do nothing
3.2.3.6   **ifend**
3.2.4   **else**
3.2.5   do nothing
3.2.6   **ifend**

Solution 5.5

The counts, *SeqCount* and *Total*, have each to be initialised to 0. *Toss* has to be given an initial value — anything other than 'Q' will do — in readiness for the first execution of step 2.1. Likewise, *PreviousToss* needs an initial value — anything other than 'H' or 'T' will do — for the first time step 3.2.3.1 is executed. In the following design, *PreviousToss* and *Toss* have been given the same initial value, but these values do not have to be the same.

1.1	$Total \leftarrow 0$
1.2	$SeqCount \leftarrow 0$
1.3	$PreviousToss \leftarrow$ 'Z'
1.4	$Toss \leftarrow$ 'Z'
2.1	**loop while** $Toss \neq$ 'Q'
3.1.1	write out "Enter H, T (or Q to quit): "
3.1.2	read in *Toss*
3.2.1	**if** $Toss \neq$ 'Q' **then**
3.2.2	$Total \leftarrow Total + 1$
3.2.3.1	**if** $Toss \neq PreviousToss$ **then**
3.2.3.2	$SeqCount \leftarrow SeqCount + 1$
3.2.3.3	$PreviousToss \leftarrow Toss$
3.2.3.4	**else**
3.2.3.5	do nothing
3.2.3.6	**ifend**
3.2.4	**else**
3.2.5	do nothing
3.2.6	**ifend**
4	**loopend**
5.1	$Mean \leftarrow Total/SeqCount$
5.2.1	write out "The mean length was "
5.2.2	write out *Mean*

Solutions to the Computer Activities

Section 1

Solution 1.1

The project CTMean1 is provided in the Block I subfolder of MT262. You can open this project (File|Open Project...) and compile it to see how a correct version of the program behaves.

You may also wish to use File|Open... to open just the code file CTMean1U.cpp so that you can compare the course team code with yours.

Solution 1.2

The course team version of the project is CTMean1x, and the code file (if you wish to open it for comparison) is CTMean1xU.cpp.

Solution 1.3

(a) A real number is accepted, but the decimal part is ignored. For example, if 3.7 is keyed in, then the machine appears to assign 3 to the integer variable concerned.

(b) Any character is accepted, but appears to be treated as if it is the integer 0.

(c) The Enter key is ignored. The program waits for you to try again, and will not move on until some acceptable key has been typed.

These answers are correct for a single error. Behaviour after an error is made is very unpredictable.

Note that what you are examining here is not your code. You are testing how *ReadIntPr* handles incorrect inputs.

Section 4

Solution 4.1

The course team version of the project is CTMean2. The code file (for comparison purposes) is CTMean2U.cpp.

Section 5

Solution 5.1

The course team version of the project is CTStats. The code file (for comparison purposes) is CTStatsU.cpp.

Index